Eternal Minds

A Hopeful Exploration of Alzheimer's Disease

By
Justin C. Wilson

Disclaimer

Table of content

Introduction

In the depths of a quiet, dimly lit room, there exists a world unfamiliar yet deeply profound. It's a world where memories flicker like distant stars, where the threads of identity seem to fray, and where the past, present, and future converge in a mysterious dance. This world is Alzheimer's disease, a condition that touches millions of lives, challenging our understanding of the human mind and the essence of humanity itself.

Welcome to "Eternal Minds," a journey through the enigmatic terrain of Alzheimer's disease. In these pages, we embark on a voyage of discovery, hope, and resilience, seeking to unravel the mysteries of a condition that has left an indelible mark on individuals, families, and societies worldwide.

We begin with the basics, delving into the intricate workings of the human brain, that marvel of nature responsible for our thoughts, memories, and emotions. Understanding the brain's elegance lays the foundation for comprehending the profound impact of Alzheimer's disease on its delicate architecture.

But Alzheimer's is not merely a story of memory loss. It's a tale of molecular complexity. We explore the intricate web of amyloid plaques, tau protein tangles, and the body's immune response that contributes to the disease's progression. We navigate the scientific frontiers where researchers tirelessly seek solutions and treatments.

In "Eternal Minds," we also intimately explore the human experience of Alzheimer's. Recognizing the early warning signs becomes a crucial skill, as we learn to empathize with those grappling with cognitive changes. We delve into the lives of caregivers, understanding their challenges and drawing inspiration from their unwavering dedication.

Yet, amidst the shadows, there's a glimmer of hope. In this section, we shine a light on the promising advances in Alzheimer's research, including clinical trials and preventive measures. We also uncover holistic approaches to care, embracing the power of lifestyle modifications, alternative therapies, and the profound mind-body connection.

As we navigate this exploration of Alzheimer's, "Eternal Minds" is not just a book; it's a testament to the enduring strength of the human spirit. It's a celebration of the resilience that shines through even in the face of profound challenges. It's a hopeful reminder that, despite the darkness of Alzheimer's, there are eternal minds within each of us, capable of kindling the light of understanding and empathy.

Join us on this voyage, for within these pages, you'll find stories of courage, breakthroughs in science, and a vision of a world where Alzheimer's disease is met with compassion, understanding, and unwavering hope. "Eternal Minds" invites you to embark on a journey of exploration and enlightenment, reminding us all that every mind, regardless of its challenges, is eternally valuable.

Chapter 1

Understanding Alzheimer's Disease

The Basics of Alzheimer's Disease

Alzheimer's disease is a progressive neurological disorder that primarily affects the brain, causing a decline in cognitive function and memory. It is the most common cause of dementia, a general term for a severe decline in cognitive ability that interferes with daily life. Here are some key points to understand about Alzheimer's:

Brain Changes: Alzheimer's is characterized by specific changes in the brain. These include the accumulation of abnormal protein deposits, such as amyloid plaques and tau tangles. These deposits interfere with the normal functioning of brain cells.

Symptoms: The early symptoms of Alzheimer's disease often include mild memory loss and difficulty with tasks that require cognitive skills. As the disease progresses, individuals may experience confusion, disorientation, language problems, and changes in behavior and personality.

Stages: Alzheimer's typically progresses through several stages, from mild cognitive impairment to moderate and severe Alzheimer's. In the later stages, individuals may require full-time care as they lose the ability to perform basic tasks like eating and bathing.

Risk Factors: While aging is the primary risk factor for Alzheimer's disease, it is not a normal part of aging. Other risk factors include genetics, family history, and certain lifestyle factors such as physical inactivity, poor diet, and cardiovascular conditions.

Diagnosis: An accurate diagnosis of Alzheimer's disease involves a comprehensive evaluation, including medical history, cognitive assessments, and sometimes brain imaging. Early diagnosis is essential to plan for future care and treatment.

Treatment: Currently, there is no cure for Alzheimer's disease. However, some medications may help manage symptoms and slow down the progression of the disease in some individuals. Non-pharmacological approaches, such as cognitive training and support for caregivers, are also crucial.

Research and Hope: Ongoing research into Alzheimer's disease aims to better understand its causes and develop more effective treatments.

Promising discoveries are being made in areas like immunotherapy and early detection.

Caregiver Challenges: Alzheimer's not only affects those diagnosed but also places significant demands on caregivers. Providing care for a loved one with Alzheimer's can be emotionally and physically challenging, requiring patience and support.

Awareness and Advocacy: Alzheimer's organizations and advocates around the world work to raise awareness, reduce stigma, and promote research funding to combat this devastating disease.

Understanding the basics of Alzheimer's disease is the first step in addressing the challenges it poses. While there is currently no cure, ongoing research offers hope for improved treatments and, ultimately, a world where Alzheimer's disease is more effectively managed and, one day, conquered.

Historical Perspective of Alzheimer's Disease

The story of Alzheimer's disease is a journey through time, marked by significant discoveries, medical breakthroughs, and a growing understanding of this complex neurological disorder. Here's a historical overview:

Early 20th Century: The Discovery by Dr. Alois Alzheimer

The history of Alzheimer's disease began in 1906 when a German psychiatrist and neuroanatomist named Dr. Alois Alzheimer examined the brain of a deceased patient named Auguste Deter. Auguste had exhibited symptoms of severe memory loss, confusion, and psychological changes during her life.

Dr. Alzheimer discovered abnormal protein deposits in Auguste's brain, including the now-famous amyloid plaques and tau tangles. This groundbreaking finding would become the hallmark of Alzheimer's disease diagnosis.

1920s to 1960s: Early Classification and Limited Understanding

In the decades following Dr. Alzheimer's discovery, medical professionals began to classify and understand the condition better. However, the disease remained relatively obscure and was often confused with other forms of dementia.

The term "Alzheimer's disease" became more widely accepted in medical literature, replacing earlier terms like "presenile dementia."

1970s to 1980s: Improved Diagnostic Techniques
Advances in medical imaging, such as computed tomography (CT) and later magnetic resonance imaging (MRI), allowed for better visualization of brain changes associated with Alzheimer's.
Researchers developed cognitive assessment tools, like the Mini-Mental State Examination (MMSE), to aid in the diagnosis and monitoring of Alzheimer's disease.

Late 20th Century: Recognition as a Major Public Health Issue
As the understanding of Alzheimer's grew, it became clear that this condition was a significant public health concern. Organizations, including the Alzheimer's Association in the United States, were founded to provide support, education, and advocacy.
The 1980s and 1990s saw the development and approval of the first medications aimed at alleviating Alzheimer's symptoms, including cholinesterase inhibitors.

21st Century: Advances in Research and Advocacy

The 21st century brought renewed focus on Alzheimer's disease, with governments, nonprofits, and research institutions worldwide investing in research and clinical trials.

Advances in genetics and biomarker research offered new insights into the underlying causes of Alzheimer's, paving the way for potential disease-modifying treatments.

Alzheimer's advocates worked tirelessly to raise awareness, reduce stigma, and promote early detection and intervention.

Present and Future: A Global Challenge

Alzheimer's disease is now recognized as a global health challenge, affecting millions of individuals and their families. The World Health Organization (WHO) acknowledges the importance of addressing dementia, including Alzheimer's, as a public health priority.

Ongoing research seeks to unravel the complexities of Alzheimer's, with the hope of developing innovative therapies and eventually finding a cure.

The historical perspective of Alzheimer's disease is a testament to the human spirit's resilience and determination to understand, combat, and ultimately conquer this devastating condition. As we look to the future, the quest to unravel the mysteries of Alzheimer's continues, offering hope for improved treatments and a world where this disease no longer casts its shadow over countless lives.

Prevalence and Impact

Prevalence of Alzheimer's Disease:
Alzheimer's disease is a global health challenge with a significant and growing prevalence. Here are key points regarding its prevalence:
Global Reach: Alzheimer's disease is not limited to any specific region or country. It affects people worldwide, making it a global concern.
Aging Population: The risk of developing Alzheimer's disease increases with age. As the global population continues to age due to improved healthcare and longer life expectancy, the prevalence of Alzheimer's is on the rise.

Statistical Data: According to estimates from the World Health Organization (WHO), as of my knowledge cutoff date in September 2021, approximately 50 million people were living with dementia worldwide, with Alzheimer's being the most common cause of dementia. This number is projected to increase significantly in the coming decades.

Economic Burden: The economic impact of Alzheimer's is substantial. The costs associated with caring for individuals with Alzheimer's, including medical expenses and caregiving, place a heavy burden on healthcare systems, families, and society as a whole.

Impact of Alzheimer's Disease:

The impact of Alzheimer's disease extends beyond individuals diagnosed with the condition and affects families, caregivers, and society in various ways:

Personal and Emotional Impact: Alzheimer's disease can profoundly affect the individuals diagnosed, leading to memory loss, confusion, changes in behavior, and a decline in cognitive function. It can also result in emotional distress and frustration.

Impact on Caregivers: Family members and friends who take on the role of caregivers for individuals with Alzheimer's face emotional, physical, and financial challenges. The demands of caregiving can lead to burnout and affect the well-being of caregivers.

Quality of Life: Alzheimer's often diminishes the quality of life for both individuals with the disease and their caregivers. Simple daily tasks become challenging, and individuals may lose the ability to recognize loved ones.

Social and Economic Impact: Alzheimer's places a significant economic burden on healthcare systems due to the high cost of care and treatment. It also impacts productivity as family members may need to reduce their work hours or leave their jobs to provide care.

Research and Advocacy: Alzheimer's has spurred research efforts to understand its causes and develop effective treatments. Advocacy organizations work to raise awareness, reduce stigma, and secure funding for research and support services.

Public Health Concern: As the prevalence of Alzheimer's continues to rise, it poses a substantial public health challenge. Governments and healthcare systems are working to address the growing needs of individuals with Alzheimer's and their families.

Hope for the Future: While Alzheimer's remains a challenging and incurable disease, ongoing research offers hope for better treatments, early detection methods, and potential disease-modifying interventions.

Alzheimer's disease is a prevalent and impactful condition that affects individuals, families, caregivers, and society as a whole. Recognizing its prevalence and understanding its far-reaching consequences is essential for promoting awareness, supporting those affected, and advancing research to improve the lives of individuals living with Alzheimer's disease.

Chapter 2

The Brain's Elegance

Anatomy and Function

Anatomy of the Human Brain:

The human brain is an incredibly complex organ composed of billions of nerve cells, neurons, and various supporting structures. It can be divided into several main regions, each with specific functions:

Cerebrum: The largest part of the brain, the cerebrum, is responsible for higher-level functions, including thinking, problem-solving, emotions, and voluntary muscle movements. It's divided into two hemispheres, the left and right, each controlling the opposite side of the body.

Cerebellum: Located at the back of the brain, the cerebellum is involved in coordinating movements, balance, and posture. It helps ensure smooth and precise motor skills.

Brainstem: The brainstem is a critical structure that connects the brain to the spinal cord. It controls vital functions like breathing, heart rate, and basic reflexes. It consists of the medulla oblongata, pons, and midbrain.

Diencephalon: This region includes the thalamus, which relays sensory information to the cerebral cortex, and the hypothalamus, responsible for regulating bodily functions like hunger, thirst, and body temperature.

Limbic System: The limbic system plays a role in emotions, memory, and behavior. It includes structures like the amygdala (emotional processing), hippocampus (memory formation), and the cingulate gyrus (emotional and cognitive processing).

Function of the Human Brain:

The human brain is responsible for a wide range of functions and activities that make us who we are:

Cognition: The cerebral cortex, particularly the frontal lobes, is responsible for higher cognitive functions such as thinking, reasoning, problem-solving, decision-making, and language.

Memory: The hippocampus, located within the limbic system, is crucial for the formation and retrieval of memories. Short-term memory and long-term memory processes involve different areas of the brain.

Motor Skills: The motor cortex in the frontal lobe controls voluntary muscle movements. The cerebellum coordinates these movements to ensure precision and smoothness.

Sensory Processing: Different areas of the brain, including the thalamus, process sensory information from our environment. This includes vision (occipital lobe), hearing (temporal lobe), touch (parietal lobe), and smell (olfactory bulb).

Emotions: The limbic system, especially the amygdala, plays a crucial role in processing emotions, including fear and pleasure.

Homeostasis: The hypothalamus regulates various bodily functions to maintain internal balance, such as body temperature, hunger, thirst, and sleep-wake cycles.

Autonomic Functions: The brainstem controls autonomic functions like heart rate, breathing, and digestion, ensuring our survival without conscious effort.

Understanding the normal anatomy and function of the human brain provides a foundation for comprehending the impact of conditions like Alzheimer's disease. In Alzheimer's, the brain experiences progressive structural and functional changes, leading to cognitive decline, memory loss, and other neurological symptoms. These changes often involve the accumulation of abnormal proteins and the disruption of neural pathways, impairing the brain's ability to perform its vital functions.

Neurons and Synapses

Let's explore the fundamental components of neurons and synapses, which are critical to understanding the workings of the brain and how Alzheimer's disease affects them:

Neurons:
Neurons, often referred to as nerve cells, are the basic building blocks of the nervous system, including the brain. They are specialized cells designed to transmit information through electrical and chemical signals. Neurons have several key components:

Cell Body (Soma): The cell body is the central part of the neuron and contains the nucleus, which houses the genetic material (DNA). It plays a role in maintaining the cell's functions.

Dendrites: Dendrites are branching extensions that receive signals from other neurons or sensory receptors. They act like antennae, gathering information from the external environment or neighboring neurons.

Axon: The axon is a long, slender projection that transmits signals away from the cell body to other neurons, muscles, or glands. It is covered by a protective myelin sheath, which enhances signal transmission.

Axon Terminals (Synaptic Terminals): At the end of the axon, there are small structures called axon terminals. These terminals contain synaptic vesicles filled with neurotransmitters, which are chemical messengers used to transmit signals to other neurons.

Synapses

Synapses are specialized junctions or connections between neurons that allow them to communicate with each other. They are essential for transmitting information throughout the nervous system. The key components of a synapse include:

Presynaptic Neuron: The neuron that sends the signal is called the presynaptic neuron. It releases neurotransmitters from its axon terminals into the synapse.

Synaptic Cleft: The synaptic cleft is a tiny gap or space between the presynaptic neuron's axon terminal and the postsynaptic neuron's dendrites or cell body.

Postsynaptic Neuron: The neuron that receives the signal is called the postsynaptic neuron. It has receptor sites on its dendrites or cell body that bind to neurotransmitters released by the presynaptic neuron.

Neurotransmitters: Neurotransmitters are chemical messengers that transmit signals across the synaptic cleft. They are released by the presynaptic neuron, travel across the gap, and bind to receptor sites on the postsynaptic neuron, thereby transmitting the signal.

The process of signal transmission at a synapse is highly dynamic and relies on the precise release and reception of neurotransmitters. When an electrical signal, known as an action potential, reaches the axon terminals of the presynaptic neuron, it triggers the release of neurotransmitters. These neurotransmitters bind to receptors on the postsynaptic neuron, leading to changes in the electrical state of the postsynaptic neuron and the propagation of the signal.

In Alzheimer's disease, one of the hallmarks is the disruption of synaptic function and the accumulation of abnormal proteins like amyloid plaques and tau tangles. These disruptions impair the ability of neurons to communicate effectively, leading to cognitive decline and memory loss, which are characteristic symptoms of the disease. Understanding the role of neurons and synapses is crucial in comprehending the impact of Alzheimer's on brain function.

The Role of Genetics

The role of genetics in Alzheimer's disease is a complex and significant aspect of understanding this condition. Here's an overview of how genetics plays a role in Alzheimer's:

Familial Alzheimer's Disease (FAD):
Some cases of Alzheimer's are directly inherited within families. This form of the disease is known as Familial Alzheimer's Disease (FAD).
FAD is caused by mutations in specific genes, such as the Amyloid Precursor Protein (APP), Presenilin 1 (PSEN1), and Presenilin 2 (PSEN2) genes.
Individuals who inherit these rare mutations have a significantly increased risk of developing Alzheimer's at a younger age, often in their 30s, 40s, or 50s.

Apolipoprotein E (APOE) Gene:
The APOE gene comes in several variations, or alleles, including APOE ε2, APOE ε3, and APOE ε4.
APOE ε4 is a known genetic risk factor for late-onset Alzheimer's disease, which is the most common form of the disease. People who inherit one copy of the APOE ε4 allele have an increased risk, while those with two copies have an even higher risk.
However, not everyone with APOE ε4 develops Alzheimer's, and many people with the disease do not have this genetic variant.

Complex Interplay of Genetics and Environment:
Alzheimer's is considered a complex, multifactorial disease, which means it results from a combination of genetic, environmental, and lifestyle factors.
While genetics can contribute to an individual's risk, other factors like age, cardiovascular health, physical activity, and education also play crucial roles in the development of the disease.

Ongoing Research and Genetic Studies:
Research into the genetics of Alzheimer's is a rapidly evolving field. Scientists are continually identifying new genetic risk factors and studying their interactions.
Large-scale genetic studies, including genome-wide association studies (GWAS), have identified multiple genetic variants associated with Alzheimer's risk.

Genetic Counseling:
Genetic testing and counseling may be offered to individuals with a family history of Alzheimer's disease, particularly those with a strong history of early-onset cases.

Genetic counseling helps individuals and families understand their genetic risk, make informed decisions, and plan for the future.

Note that while genetics plays a role in Alzheimer's disease, it is not the sole determinant. Environmental and lifestyle factors, as well as random genetic mutations, also contribute to an individual's risk. Additionally, ongoing research aims to better understand the genetic underpinnings of Alzheimer's, which may lead to improved diagnostic tools and potential treatments in the future.

If you have concerns about your genetic risk for Alzheimer's disease or a family history of the condition, it's advisable to consult with a genetic counselor or healthcare professional who can provide personalized guidance and information based on your specific situation.

Chapter 3

Alzheimer's Disease: A Molecular Puzzle

Amyloid Plaques

Amyloid plaques are abnormal protein deposits that accumulate in the brains of individuals with Alzheimer's disease. These plaques are a hallmark feature of the disease and play a central role in its pathology. Here's an overview of amyloid plaques and their significance in Alzheimer's:

Composition:

Amyloid plaques primarily consist of a protein called beta-amyloid ($A\beta$). Beta-amyloid is a fragment of a larger protein called the amyloid precursor protein (APP).

In Alzheimer's disease, abnormal processing of APP leads to the production of beta-amyloid molecules that tend to aggregate and form plaques.

Accumulation in the Brain:

Amyloid plaques accumulate in various regions of the brain, particularly in the cerebral cortex, which is involved in higher cognitive functions.
Over time, these plaques can become dense and widespread, interfering with normal brain function.

Role in Alzheimer's Pathology:
While the precise role of amyloid plaques in Alzheimer's disease is still the subject of ongoing research, they are believed to contribute to the disease's progression in several ways:

- Neurotoxicity: Beta-amyloid aggregates can be toxic to neurons (nerve cells), leading to their dysfunction and death.

- Disruption of Synapses: Amyloid plaques can disrupt synaptic function, impairing communication between neurons.

- Inflammation: The presence of amyloid plaques can trigger an inflammatory response in the brain, further damaging neurons.

Connection to Tau Tangles:
Amyloid plaques are often found in conjunction with another hallmark of Alzheimer's disease, which is tau protein tangles (neurofibrillary tangles).

Tau tangles are abnormal clumps of tau protein inside neurons and are closely linked to neuronal dysfunction.

Diagnostic Significance:
Amyloid imaging using positron emission tomography (PET) scans and cerebrospinal fluid analysis of beta-amyloid levels are diagnostic tools used to identify the presence of amyloid plaques in living individuals.
The presence of amyloid plaques is considered a key biomarker for Alzheimer's disease.

Target for Research and Treatment:
Amyloid plaques have been a major focus of Alzheimer's research. Many drug trials have aimed to target and reduce amyloid plaque accumulation in the brain as a potential treatment strategy.
While some therapies have shown promise in reducing amyloid levels, their effectiveness in slowing or halting disease progression remains a subject of ongoing investigation.
Note that amyloid plaques are just one part of the complex puzzle of Alzheimer's disease, and their exact role in the development and progression of the condition continues to be studied. Alzheimer's is a

multifactorial disease with contributions from various genetic, environmental, and molecular factors, and researchers are working diligently to uncover more about its underlying mechanisms and potential treatment approaches.

Tau Protein Tangles

Tau protein tangles, also known as neurofibrillary tangles (NFTs), are abnormal clumps of tau protein that accumulate inside neurons (nerve cells) in the brains of individuals with Alzheimer's disease and certain other neurodegenerative disorders. Tau protein plays a crucial role in the normal functioning of neurons, particularly in maintaining the stability of microtubules, which are essential components of the neuronal cytoskeleton. Here's an overview of tau protein tangles and their significance in Alzheimer's disease:

Formation of Tau Tangles:
Tau is a protein naturally found in neurons, where it helps maintain the structural integrity and stability of microtubules. In Alzheimer's disease, tau proteins

become abnormally modified and lose their ability to bind to microtubules.

As a result, tau proteins aggregate and accumulate within neurons, forming twisted and tangled structures known as neurofibrillary tangles.

Location in the Brain:

Tau tangles are typically found in the regions of the brain that are critical for memory, learning, and cognitive functions. These regions include the hippocampus and the cerebral cortex.

The presence of tau tangles contributes to the disruption of neural circuits and, ultimately, cognitive decline.

Impact on Neuronal Function:

The accumulation of tau tangles disrupts the normal functioning of neurons in several ways:

- Neuronal Dysfunction: Tau tangles interfere with the transport of essential molecules and nutrients within neurons, leading to cellular dysfunction.

-Neuronal Death: Over time, the presence of tau tangles can cause neuronal death, contributing to the progressive loss of brain tissue seen in Alzheimer's disease.

-Impaired Signaling: Tau pathology disrupts the communication between neurons, impairing memory and cognitive functions.

Relationship with Beta-Amyloid Plaques:

Tau tangles are often found in conjunction with another hallmark of Alzheimer's disease: beta-amyloid plaques.

While the exact relationship between tau and beta-amyloid in Alzheimer's pathology is still an active area of research, it is clear that both contribute to neuronal dysfunction and cognitive decline.

Diagnostic Significance:

Tau pathology, including the presence of tau tangles, is a key neuropathological hallmark of Alzheimer's disease.

Imaging techniques, such as positron emission tomography (PET) scans, can detect abnormal tau protein in the living brain, aiding in the diagnosis and monitoring of Alzheimer's disease.

Target for Research and Treatment:

Understanding the role of tau pathology has become a major focus of Alzheimer's research. Efforts are underway to develop therapies that target tau pathology in addition to beta-amyloid.

Several drug candidates are in clinical trials aimed at reducing or removing tau tangles as a potential treatment strategy.

Tau protein tangles are a significant component of Alzheimer's disease pathology, and their contribution to neuronal dysfunction and cognitive decline underscores the complex nature of this devastating neurodegenerative disorder. Researchers continue to investigate tau-related mechanisms and potential therapeutic interventions to address the impact of tau pathology in Alzheimer's disease.

Inflammation and Immune Response

Inflammation and the immune response are integral aspects of the body's defense mechanisms. They play a crucial role in Alzheimer's disease, both as a response to the disease's pathology and as a potential contributor to its progression. Here's an overview of inflammation and the immune response in the context of Alzheimer's:

Inflammation in Alzheimer's Disease:

Inflammation is the body's natural response to injury, infection, or harmful stimuli. It is a complex process involving various immune cells, signaling molecules, and biochemical pathways.

In Alzheimer's disease, chronic inflammation in the brain is often observed. This inflammation is believed to be triggered, at least in part, by the accumulation of beta-amyloid plaques and tau protein tangles.

Role of Microglia:

Microglia are specialized immune cells in the brain that act as the first line of defense against infections and injuries. They also play a role in monitoring and maintaining the brain's environment.

In Alzheimer's, microglia can become activated in response to the presence of beta-amyloid plaques and tau tangles. Activated microglia release inflammatory molecules.

Immune Response in the Brain:

While inflammation and immune responses are typically protective, in Alzheimer's disease, they can become dysregulated.

Chronic inflammation in the brain can lead to the release of pro-inflammatory cytokines and chemokines, which can damage neurons and contribute to neurodegeneration.

Blood-Brain Barrier (BBB):
The blood-brain barrier is a protective barrier that separates the bloodstream from the brain and spinal cord. It regulates the entry of substances, including immune cells and molecules, into the brain.
In Alzheimer's, there is evidence that the blood-brain barrier can become compromised, allowing immune cells from the bloodstream to enter the brain, potentially exacerbating inflammation.

Potential Consequences:
The chronic inflammation seen in Alzheimer's disease is thought to contribute to neuronal damage and cognitive decline.
Inflammation can lead to the production of reactive oxygen species (ROS) and oxidative stress, which can further harm neurons and other brain cells.

Therapeutic Approaches:

Researchers are exploring various therapeutic approaches to modulate the immune response and reduce inflammation in Alzheimer's.

Anti-inflammatory drugs, such as nonsteroidal anti-inflammatory drugs (NSAIDs), have been investigated, although their effectiveness in slowing or halting disease progression remains a subject of study.

Ongoing Research:

The role of inflammation and the immune response in Alzheimer's disease is an active area of research. Scientists are working to better understand the precise mechanisms involved and to develop targeted therapies that can modulate these responses without compromising their essential protective functions.

inflammation and the immune response in Alzheimer's disease represent a complex interplay of protective and potentially harmful processes. While the immune system's activation is a natural response to the disease's pathology, chronic and dysregulated inflammation can contribute to neurodegeneration and cognitive decline. Understanding these processes is essential for developing potential treatments that can modulate the immune response in Alzheimer's without causing harm.

Chapter 4

Early Warning Signs

Recognizing Cognitive Changes

Recognizing cognitive changes, especially in yourself or a loved one, is essential for early detection and intervention in conditions like Alzheimer's disease. Here are some common signs to be aware of:

Memory Loss:
Forgetting recently learned information, important dates, or events. Repeatedly asking for the same information or relying on memory aids.

Difficulty Planning and Problem-Solving:
Finding it challenging to develop and follow a plan or solve everyday problems.

Confusion with Time or Place:
Losing track of dates, seasons, or the passage of time.

Becoming disoriented and not recognizing familiar locations or environments.

Trouble with Visual and Spatial Relationships:
Difficulty reading, judging distance, or determining color and contrast.
Problems with coordination and balance.

Language Problems:
Struggling with vocabulary, such as calling things by the wrong name.
Repeating oneself or having difficulty following or joining a conversation.

Misplacing Items:
Putting things in unusual places, like placing keys in the refrigerator.
Being unable to retrace steps to find lost items.

Decreased Judgment:
Poor decision-making, such as giving away large sums of money to telemarketers or neglecting personal hygiene.

Social Withdrawal:
Pulling away from hobbies, social activities, work, or sports that were once enjoyed.
Avoiding social interaction due to the fear of cognitive difficulties.

Personality and Mood Changes:
Experiencing mood swings, including increased irritability, confusion, or depression.
Changes in personality, such as becoming more anxious or suspicious.

Decline in Work or Social Functioning:
Finding it challenging to complete familiar tasks at work or home.
 Struggling to understand or follow social norms and engage in conversations.
Occasional memory lapses or difficulties in cognitive function can occur as a natural part of aging and might not necessarily indicate a cognitive disorder like Alzheimer's. However, persistent and worsening symptoms that interfere with daily life and activities should be discussed with a healthcare professional for a thorough evaluation.
Early detection and diagnosis of cognitive changes are crucial, as they may provide an opportunity for

interventions, treatments, and support that can enhance the quality of life for individuals affected by cognitive disorders. If you or a loved one are concerned about cognitive changes, don't hesitate to seek medical advice and evaluation.

Diagnosis and Staging

Diagnosis and staging of Alzheimer's disease involve a comprehensive evaluation to confirm the presence of the condition, determine its severity, and plan for appropriate care and support. Here's an overview of the diagnostic process and stages of Alzheimer's disease:

Diagnosis of Alzheimer's Disease:

Medical History and Clinical Assessment: The diagnostic process often begins with a thorough medical history and clinical assessment. The healthcare provider will discuss symptoms, medical history, and any family history of dementia.

Cognitive and Functional Assessments: Cognitive assessments, such as the Mini-Mental State Examination (MMSE) or the Montreal Cognitive Assessment (MoCA), are used to evaluate memory, thinking, and problem-solving abilities. Functional assessments assess an individual's ability to perform daily activities independently.

Laboratory Tests: Blood tests are typically performed to rule out other medical conditions that could cause cognitive impairment, such as thyroid disorders or vitamin deficiencies.

Neuroimaging: Brain imaging techniques like magnetic resonance imaging (MRI) and positron emission tomography (PET) scans can help detect brain changes, including the presence of beta-amyloid plaques and tau tangles.

Cerebrospinal Fluid Analysis: In some cases, cerebrospinal fluid analysis may be performed to measure levels of beta-amyloid and tau proteins, which are associated with Alzheimer's.

Genetic Testing: Genetic testing may be considered in cases of early-onset Alzheimer's or when there is a strong family history of the disease.

Staging of Alzheimer's Disease:
Alzheimer's disease is often staged to help understand its progression and plan appropriate care and support. Various staging systems exist, but one commonly used system is the Global Deterioration Scale (GDS) or the Clinical Dementia Rating (CDR) scale. These scales generally describe the disease's progression in the following stages:

Stage 1: No Cognitive Decline (GDS 1): In the earliest stage, there are no significant cognitive impairments. Memory and cognitive functions are normal.

Stage 2: Very Mild Cognitive Decline (GDS 2): At this stage, individuals may experience minor memory lapses that are typical with aging. These lapses do not significantly interfere with daily life.

Stage 3: Mild Cognitive Decline (GDS 3): Mild cognitive impairment becomes noticeable. Individuals may have difficulty finding words, remembering names, or performing complex tasks.

Stage 4: Moderate Cognitive Decline (GDS 4): In this stage, individuals experience clear cognitive deficits, including trouble with memory, solving problems, and managing finances. Daily life activities are affected.

Stage 5: Moderately Severe Cognitive Decline (GDS 5): Individuals require assistance with daily activities like dressing and bathing. They may become disoriented to time and place.

Stage 6: Severe Cognitive Decline (GDS 6): Severe memory loss, personality changes, and an inability to recognize loved ones are common in this stage. Assistance is needed for most daily tasks.

Stage 7: Very Severe Cognitive Decline (GDS 7): In the final stage, individuals lose the ability to communicate, control movements, and respond to the environment. Full-time care is required.

Alzheimer's disease progression can vary widely among individuals, and not everyone experiences all of these stages. Additionally, the diagnostic and staging process may involve input from multiple healthcare professionals, including neurologists, geriatricians, and neuropsychologists, to ensure accurate assessment and personalized care planning. Early diagnosis allows for interventions and support that can improve the quality of life for individuals with Alzheimer's and their caregivers.

Chapter 5

Living with Alzheimer's

Coping Strategies

Coping with Alzheimer's disease, whether you're a person living with the condition or a caregiver, can be challenging, but there are effective strategies to help manage the journey. Here are some coping strategies:

For Individuals Living with Alzheimer's:
Stay Organized: Use calendars, reminder apps, or written notes to help keep track of appointments, medications, and daily tasks.

Maintain a Routine: Establishing a daily routine can provide structure and reduce anxiety. Consistency in activities can help you feel more comfortable.

Engage in Cognitive Activities: Stay mentally active with puzzles, games, reading, or hobbies that you enjoy. This can help maintain cognitive function.

Physical Activity: Regular exercise has been shown to have cognitive benefits. Consult with your healthcare provider for safe and appropriate exercise options.

Healthy Diet: Eating a balanced diet rich in fruits, vegetables, whole grains, and lean proteins can support overall health.

Seek Social Support: Stay connected with friends and family members. Engaging in social activities can provide emotional support and reduce feelings of isolation.

Accept Help: Don't hesitate to ask for assistance when needed. Accepting help from caregivers or support services can ease daily challenges.

Practice Stress Reduction: Techniques like meditation, deep breathing, and relaxation exercises can help reduce stress and anxiety.

For Caregivers:

Education: Learn as much as you can about Alzheimer's disease to understand what to expect and how to provide the best care.

Seek Support: Join support groups for caregivers or seek professional counseling to manage stress and emotions.

Respite Care: Take regular breaks to rest and recharge. Respite care services can provide temporary relief and allow you to focus on self-care.

Effective Communication: Practice clear and patient communication with your loved one. Use simple, direct language and maintain eye contact.

Safety Precautions: Ensure the home environment is safe, with measures like removing tripping hazards and installing handrails as needed.

Medication Management: Keep track of medication schedules, and consult with healthcare providers for any changes or concerns.

Empathy and Compassion: Understand that behaviors and moods may change due to the disease. Approach caregiving with empathy and compassion.

Plan for the Future: Discuss and plan for future care needs, legal matters, and financial decisions while your loved one can still participate in decision-making.

self-care: Prioritize your well-being. Caregiver burnout is common, so make time for activities that rejuvenate you.

Celebrate Small Wins: Recognize and celebrate even small achievements and moments of joy in your caregiving journey.

Note that Alzheimer's disease is a progressive condition, and it's okay to seek help and support. Engaging with healthcare professionals, support groups, and community resources can make the caregiving journey more manageable.

Additionally, each person's experience with Alzheimer's is unique, so adapt these strategies to fit your specific situation and needs. Alzheimer's associations and organizations often provide valuable resources, information, and support to individuals and caregivers dealing with the disease.

Caregiver Perspectives

Caregiving for a loved one with Alzheimer's disease is both rewarding and challenging. Caregivers play a crucial role in providing support and maintaining the quality of life for individuals with Alzheimer's. Here are some caregiver perspectives on their experiences:

Unconditional Love: Many caregivers emphasize the deep love and emotional connection they have with their loved one with Alzheimer's. They see caregiving as an expression of that love.

Emotional Rollercoaster: Caregivers often describe the emotional toll of the role. They may experience a range of emotions, including sadness, frustration, guilt, and grief, as they witness the changes in their loved ones.

Patience and Adaptability: Caregivers learn the importance of patience and adaptability. They adapt to their loved one's changing abilities and find new ways to communicate and connect.

Finding Joy in Small Moments: Caregivers often find joy in small moments of connection and recognition, even when their loved one's memory is fading. These moments become cherished memories.

Self-Care Challenges: Balancing caregiving responsibilities with self-care can be difficult. Many caregivers struggle with feelings of guilt when taking time for themselves.

Advocacy and Support: Caregivers often become advocates for their loved ones, ensuring they receive the best care and support. They may join support groups and seek resources to navigate the healthcare system.

Long-Term Commitment: Caregiving for someone with Alzheimer's is a long-term commitment. Caregivers face the challenge of adapting to evolving care needs over time.

Moments of Resilience: Caregivers demonstrate remarkable resilience in the face of adversity. They continue to provide care despite the challenges and setbacks.

Educational Journey: Many caregivers become experts in Alzheimer's disease, learning about the condition, treatments, and effective caregiving techniques.

Celebrating Life: Caregivers often focus on celebrating the life of their loved one rather than dwelling solely on the challenges of the disease. They create meaningful experiences and memories.

Need for Support: Caregivers stress the importance of seeking support from friends, family, and support groups. They acknowledge that caregiving is a shared responsibility.

Empathy and Compassion: Caregivers express empathy and compassion for their loved ones, recognizing that Alzheimer's is a difficult journey for both the individual with the disease and the caregiver.

It's essential to recognize the incredible dedication and resilience of caregivers in the Alzheimer's community. Their unwavering support and commitment make a significant difference in the lives of those living with the disease. Providing support and resources for caregivers is vital to help them navigate the challenges of Alzheimer's disease caregiving effectively.

Support and Resources

Support and resources are essential for individuals living with Alzheimer's disease and their caregivers. Here are some valuable sources of support and resources:

Alzheimer's Associations and Organizations: Organizations like the Alzheimer's Association (in the United States) and Alzheimer's Society (in the United Kingdom) offer a wealth of information, support groups, and resources for both individuals with Alzheimer's and caregivers.

Healthcare Professionals: Consult with healthcare providers, including neurologists, geriatricians, and social workers, who can provide guidance, diagnosis, and information about treatment options.

Support Groups: Joining caregiver support groups or Alzheimer 's-specific support groups can provide emotional support, practical advice, and a sense of community with others facing similar challenges.

Respite Care Services: Respite care services provide temporary relief for caregivers, allowing them to take breaks and recharge. These services may be offered through local agencies or organizations.

In-Home Care Services: Professional caregivers can assist with daily activities, provide companionship, and ensure the safety and well-being of individuals with Alzheimer's while allowing them to remain in their homes.

Adult Day Care Programs: Adult day care centers offer supervised activities, social interaction, and medical monitoring for individuals with Alzheimer's, providing caregivers with much-needed respite during the day.

Legal and Financial Planning: Consult with an attorney or financial advisor to address legal matters such as power of attorney, advance directives, and financial planning to ensure the future well-being of the person with Alzheimer's.

Memory Care Facilities: Memory care facilities are specialized care settings designed for individuals with Alzheimer's or other forms of dementia. These facilities provide 24/7 care and support.

Educational Resources: Access educational materials, books, and online resources that provide information about Alzheimer's disease, caregiving techniques, and coping strategies.

Assistive Technologies: Explore assistive technologies, such as tracking devices, medication reminders, and safety alarms, to help manage daily tasks and ensure safety.

Government and Community Programs: Many governments offer programs and services for individuals with Alzheimer's and their caregivers. Check with local government agencies and community organizations for available support.

Hospice Care: Hospice care services provide end-of-life care and support for individuals with advanced Alzheimer's. Hospice professionals focus on comfort and quality of life.

Telehealth Services: Telehealth services can provide remote access to healthcare professionals, which can be especially valuable for individuals with Alzheimer's and their caregivers who may face mobility challenges.

Support from Friends and Family: Don't underestimate the importance of support from friends and family members. Enlist their help and create a caregiving network to share responsibilities and provide emotional support.

Navigating the challenges of Alzheimer's disease requires a multidisciplinary approach and a strong support system. Remember that you are not alone, and there are many resources available to help you and your loved one through this journey. Reaching out for support and information is a proactive step toward providing the best possible care and maintaining the quality of life for everyone involved.

Chapter 6

Advances in Alzheimer's Research

Promising Discoveries

Research into Alzheimer's disease has led to several promising discoveries and ongoing investigations that hold the potential for better understanding, diagnosing, and treating the condition. Here are some of the promising developments in Alzheimer's research:

Early Biomarkers: Researchers are making progress in identifying biomarkers, such as specific proteins or molecules in the blood or cerebrospinal fluid, that can detect Alzheimer's disease in its early stages. This can lead to earlier and more accurate diagnosis.

Advancements in Imaging: Imaging techniques like positron emission tomography (PET) scans and magnetic resonance imaging (MRI) are continually improving, allowing for better visualization of brain changes associated with Alzheimer's.

Anti-Amyloid and Anti-Tau Therapies: Several drug candidates targeting beta-amyloid and tau proteins, which are hallmarks of Alzheimer's, are in clinical trials. These therapies aim to slow or halt disease progression.

Immunotherapy: Immunotherapies that stimulate the immune system to clear amyloid plaques are showing promise in clinical trials.

Lifestyle Interventions: Research suggests that lifestyle factors such as diet, exercise, cognitive stimulation, and social engagement may help reduce the risk of Alzheimer's and slow its progression.

Precision Medicine: The field of precision medicine aims to tailor treatments to an individual's unique genetic and molecular profile. This approach holds the potential for more personalized Alzheimer's care.

Cognitive Training: Cognitive training programs and digital tools are being developed to help individuals with Alzheimer's and mild cognitive impairment improve cognitive function and maintain independence.

Supportive Therapies: Research continues into supportive therapies that address symptoms and improve quality of life, such as sleep management, pain relief, and behavioral interventions.

Brain Health Initiatives: Public health campaigns and initiatives are raising awareness about brain health and the importance of preventive measures to reduce Alzheimer's risk.

Collaborative Research Efforts: Collaborative efforts between researchers, pharmaceutical companies, and government agencies are accelerating progress in Alzheimer's research.

Alzheimer's research is a complex and ongoing endeavor, and not all promising discoveries lead to effective treatments. However, these advancements offer hope for the future and underscore the dedication of scientists and healthcare professionals working toward a better understanding of Alzheimer's disease and improved outcomes for individuals and families affected by it. Continued support for research, clinical trials, and public awareness is essential to drive progress in the field.

Clinical Trials and Treatments

Clinical trials play a critical role in the development and testing of potential treatments for Alzheimer's disease. While there is currently no cure for Alzheimer's, ongoing research aims to find ways to slow its progression, alleviate symptoms, and improve the quality of life for individuals living with the disease. Here's an overview of clinical trials and some emerging treatments:

Clinical Trials:

Phases of Clinical Trials: Clinical trials typically progress through several phases:

- Phase 1: Initial testing of a new treatment in a small group of people to assess safety.

- Phase 2: Testing in a larger group to evaluate effectiveness and further assess safety.

- Phase 3: Large-scale testing to confirm effectiveness, monitor side effects, and compare the treatment to standard treatments or a placebo.

- Phase 4: Post-marketing studies to gather additional information about long-term safety and effectiveness.

Types of Trials: Alzheimer's clinical trials can involve various approaches, including drug trials targeting beta-amyloid and tau proteins, immunotherapies, cognitive interventions, and lifestyle interventions.

Participation: Participation in clinical trials is voluntary. Individuals with Alzheimer's, caregivers, and healthy volunteers can participate. Participation can provide access to experimental treatments and contribute to advancing Alzheimer's research.

Trial Registries: Organizations like the Alzheimer's Association and clinicaltrials.gov provide information on ongoing clinical trials and how to participate.

Emerging Treatments: Anti-Amyloid and Anti-Tau Therapies:

Several drugs targeting beta-amyloid and tau proteins are in clinical trials. Some focus on reducing the production of these proteins, while others aim to clear existing plaques and tangles.

Immunotherapies: Immunotherapies stimulate the immune system to target beta-amyloid plaques. Some have shown promise in early-stage trials.

Lifestyle Interventions: Research suggests that adopting a healthy lifestyle, including a balanced diet, physical activity, mental stimulation, and social engagement, may help reduce Alzheimer's risk and slow its progression.

Cognitive Interventions: Cognitive training programs and digital interventions are being developed to improve cognitive function in individuals with Alzheimer's.

Supportive Therapies: Medications and interventions are available to manage symptoms like sleep disturbances, agitation, and mood changes.

Precision Medicine: The concept of precision medicine involves tailoring treatments to an individual's unique genetic and molecular profile. This approach is being explored in Alzheimer's research.

while promising treatments are in development, not all experimental therapies prove effective in later-stage clinical trials. The Alzheimer's research community continues to work tirelessly to advance our understanding of the disease and develop effective treatments.

If you or a loved one is interested in participating in a clinical trial, consult with healthcare providers and researchers to find an appropriate trial. Participating in research can contribute to the collective effort to combat Alzheimer's disease and improve the lives of those affected by it.

Preventive Measures

Preventive measures and lifestyle choices can play a significant role in reducing the risk of Alzheimer's disease and promoting brain health. While there is no guaranteed way to prevent Alzheimer's, adopting a combination of these strategies may help lower the risk:

Stay Mentally Active: Engage in cognitive activities that challenge your brain, such as puzzles, crosswords, reading, learning a new skill, or playing musical instruments.

Maintain a Healthy Diet: Eat a balanced diet rich in fruits, vegetables, whole grains, lean proteins, and healthy fats. Some studies suggest that diets like the Mediterranean diet may be beneficial for brain health.

Regular Physical Exercise: Aim for regular physical activity, such as brisk walking, swimming, or dancing. Exercise has been shown to improve blood flow to the brain and may reduce the risk of cognitive decline.

Manage Cardiovascular Health: Conditions like high blood pressure, diabetes, and high cholesterol can increase the risk of Alzheimer's. Manage these conditions through medication and lifestyle changes.

Social Engagement: Stay socially active by maintaining relationships, participating in social activities, and connecting with friends and family. Social engagement is linked to better cognitive health.

Get Quality Sleep: Prioritize good sleep hygiene. Aim for 7-9 hours of quality sleep per night. Poor sleep can contribute to cognitive problems.

Mental Health and Stress Reduction: Manage stress through relaxation techniques, mindfulness, or meditation. Mental health conditions like depression can increase Alzheimer's risk, so seek treatment if needed.

Stay Physically Active: Engage in regular physical activity to improve blood flow to the brain, reduce inflammation, and support overall brain health.

Brain-Boosting Activities: Engage in activities that stimulate your mind, such as learning a new language, taking up a musical instrument, or pursuing creative hobbies.

Limit Alcohol Consumption: If you consume alcohol, do so in moderation. Excessive alcohol intake can harm brain health.

Avoid Smoking: Smoking is associated with an increased risk of cognitive decline. Quitting smoking can have significant health benefits.

Protect Your Head: Prevent head injuries by wearing seat belts in cars, using helmets when cycling, and taking precautions to avoid falls.

Regular Check-Ups: Schedule regular check-ups with your healthcare provider to monitor overall health and address any medical conditions or concerns promptly.

Stay Mentally Active: Engage in lifelong learning. Challenging your mind with new experiences and knowledge may help preserve cognitive function.

Note that while these preventive measures can contribute to overall brain health and may reduce the risk of cognitive decline, they are not guarantees against Alzheimer's disease. Genetics and other factors also play a role. Consult with healthcare professionals for personalized advice and to address specific health concerns.

Chapter 7

Holistic Approaches to Alzheimer's Care

Lifestyle Modifications

Lifestyle modifications can have a positive impact on overall health and well-being, including brain health and potentially reducing the risk of Alzheimer's disease. Here are some lifestyle modifications to consider:

Diet: Adopt a brain-healthy diet rich in fruits, vegetables, whole grains, lean proteins, and healthy fats. Consider the Mediterranean diet, which is associated with cognitive benefits.

Physical Activity: Engage in regular physical exercise. Aim for at least 150 minutes of moderate-intensity aerobic activity per week. Exercise improves blood flow to the brain and can support cognitive health.

Mental Stimulation: Keep your mind active with activities that challenge cognitive function. Solve puzzles, play brain games, learn new skills, or engage in creative hobbies.

Social Engagement: Stay socially connected with friends and family. Engage in social activities, join clubs, or volunteer. Social interactions are beneficial for brain health.

Sleep Hygiene: Prioritize good sleep hygiene by maintaining a consistent sleep schedule and creating a comfortable sleep environment. Aim for 7-9 hours of quality sleep per night.

Stress Management: Practice stress-reduction techniques such as mindfulness, meditation, yoga, or deep breathing exercises. Chronic stress can negatively affect brain health.

Quit Smoking: If you smoke, seek support and quit smoking. Smoking is linked to cognitive decline and an increased risk of Alzheimer's.

Limit Alcohol: If you consume alcohol, do so in moderation. Excessive alcohol intake can harm brain health.

Manage Chronic Health Conditions: Effectively manage chronic conditions like high blood pressure, diabetes, and high cholesterol through medication and lifestyle changes.

Protect Your Head: Wear seat belts in cars, use helmets when cycling or engaging in activities that pose a head injury risk, and take precautions to prevent falls.

Medication Management: If you are on medication, follow your healthcare provider's instructions for proper management and adhere to your medication regimen.

Regular Check-Ups: Schedule regular check-ups with your healthcare provider to monitor your overall health and address any medical conditions or concerns.

Brain-Boosting Activities: Engage in activities that stimulate your mind, such as learning a new language, taking up a musical instrument, or pursuing creative hobbies.

Maintain a Healthy Weight: Aim for a healthy body weight through a combination of a balanced diet and regular exercise. Obesity is associated with an increased risk of cognitive decline.

Lifestyle modifications are most effective when implemented as part of a comprehensive approach to overall health and well-being. Consult with healthcare professionals for personalized guidance and recommendations tailored to your specific needs and circumstances.

Alternative therapies

While there is no cure for Alzheimer's disease, some alternative therapies and complementary approaches may be considered to help manage symptoms and improve the overall well-being of individuals with Alzheimer's. It's important to note that these therapies should be used in conjunction with conventional medical care and under the guidance of healthcare professionals. Here are some alternative therapies and approaches to consider:

Music Therapy: Music therapy involves listening to or playing music, which can have a calming and mood-enhancing effect. It may help improve emotional well-being and cognitive function in individuals with Alzheimer's.

Art Therapy Art therapy allows individuals to express themselves through art, such as painting, drawing, or sculpting. It can be a creative outlet and a means of communication for those who have difficulty with verbal expression.

Pet Therapy: Interactions with therapy animals, such as dogs or cats, can provide comfort and reduce anxiety. Pet therapy may also stimulate social engagement and improve mood.

Aromatherapy: Aromatherapy involves the use of scents and essential oils to promote relaxation and reduce stress. Certain scents may have a calming effect and enhance well-being.

Massage Therapy: Gentle massage can help relax individuals with Alzheimer's and reduce feelings of anxiety and agitation. It may also improve circulation and ease muscle tension.

Acupuncture: Acupuncture is a traditional Chinese therapy involving the insertion of fine needles at specific points on the body. Some individuals find it helpful for managing stress and promoting relaxation.

Light Therapy: Exposure to natural light or specially designed light boxes may help regulate sleep patterns and reduce symptoms of depression in individuals with Alzheimer's.

Herbal and Dietary Supplements: Some individuals explore the use of herbal supplements or dietary modifications to support cognitive function or reduce symptoms. It's important to consult with a healthcare provider before using any supplements, as they may interact with medications.

Mind-Body Practices: Mindfulness meditation, yoga, and tai chi are mind-body practices that may promote relaxation, reduce stress, and enhance overall well-being.

Cognitive Stimulation Therapy: Structured cognitive stimulation programs involve activities and exercises designed to engage cognitive function and improve memory and thinking skills.

Environmental Modifications: Creating a calming and familiar environment can help reduce confusion and agitation in individuals with Alzheimer's. This may include using color-coded cues, minimizing clutter, and providing clear signage.

It's crucial to approach alternative therapies with caution and consider individual preferences and needs. Consult with healthcare professionals, such as physicians, neurologists, or geriatric specialists, before implementing any alternative therapies. They can guide the safety and appropriateness of these approaches and ensure they complement the overall care plan for Alzheimer's disease.

Mind-Body Connection

The mind-body connection refers to the intricate relationship between a person's mental and emotional state (mind) and their physical health and well-being (body). It suggests that the two are interconnected and can influence each other significantly. Here are some key aspects of the mind-body connection:

Stress and Physical Health: High levels of stress and chronic stress can have a detrimental impact on physical health. It can lead to various health issues, including cardiovascular problems, digestive disorders, and a weakened immune system.

Emotional Well-Being: Positive emotions, such as happiness and contentment, can promote physical well-being. Conversely, negative emotions like depression and anxiety can contribute to physical health problems.

Immune System: The immune system can be influenced by emotional states. Chronic stress, for example, can weaken the immune system's ability to defend against infections and illnesses.

Pain Perception: Emotional well-being can affect how individuals perceive and cope with pain. For example, stress and anxiety can amplify the perception of pain, while relaxation techniques can reduce it.

Cognitive Function: Mental health and cognitive function are closely connected. Emotional well-being and effective stress management can positively impact memory, concentration, and problem-solving abilities.

Lifestyle Choices: Emotional states can influence lifestyle choices, such as eating habits, physical activity, and sleep patterns. Positive emotions may lead to healthier choices, while negative emotions can result in less healthy behaviors.

Mindfulness and Relaxation: Mindfulness practices, meditation, and relaxation techniques can help individuals manage stress and improve overall well-being. These practices focus on the mind-body connection by promoting relaxation and reducing physical and emotional tension.

Psychosomatic Illnesses: Some illnesses are believed to have a strong mind-body connection, where emotional factors contribute to physical symptoms. Conditions like irritable bowel syndrome (IBS) and tension headaches are examples.

Placebo Effect: The placebo effect demonstrates the power of belief and expectation on physical health. Individuals may experience improvements in symptoms simply because they believe they are receiving treatment.

Holistic Health: Holistic approaches to health consider the mind and body as interconnected parts of overall well-being. These approaches aim to promote balance and harmony between mental and physical health.

Resilience and Coping: A strong mind-body connection can enhance an individual's ability to cope with challenges and bounce back from adversity. Resilience involves emotional and physical elements.

Understanding the mind-body connection is essential for promoting overall health and well-being. Practices that strengthen this connection, such as mindfulness, stress management, and emotional self-awareness, can have a positive impact on both mental and physical health. It's a reminder that taking care of your emotional and mental health is just as crucial as caring for your physical health.

Chapter 8

The Power of Advocacy

Raising Awareness

Raising awareness about Alzheimer's disease is crucial to increase understanding, reduce stigma, promote early detection, and support individuals living with the condition and their caregivers. Here are some effective ways to raise awareness about Alzheimer's:

Education and Information: Organize workshops, webinars, or public talks to provide information about Alzheimer's disease, its symptoms, risk factors, and available resources.

Community Events: Host community events, such as walks, runs, or fundraisers, to engage people and raise funds for Alzheimer's research and support services.

Social Media Campaigns: Utilize social media platforms to share informative content, personal stories, and statistics about Alzheimer's. Use relevant hashtags to reach a wider audience.

Personal Stories: Encourage individuals and families affected by Alzheimer's to share their personal stories and experiences. Real-life stories can be powerful tools for raising awareness and reducing stigma.

Advocacy and Policy Change: Get involved in advocacy efforts to influence government policies related to Alzheimer's research funding, caregiver support, and healthcare access.

Collaborate with Alzheimer's Associations: Partner with local or national Alzheimer's associations to leverage their resources and reach a broader audience.

Dementia-Friendly Communities: Promote the creation of dementia-friendly communities that provide support, understanding, and accessible services for individuals with Alzheimer's and their caregivers.

Healthcare Provider Engagement: Work with healthcare providers to ensure they are informed about the latest developments in Alzheimer's research and can provide appropriate guidance to patients and families.

Schools and Education: Introduce Alzheimer's education into school curricula to increase awareness among younger generations.

Volunteer Opportunities: Encourage community members to volunteer their time and skills to support individuals with Alzheimer's and their caregivers.

Media Coverage: Reach out to local media outlets to cover Alzheimer 's-related stories, events, and initiatives to reach a broader audience.

International Alzheimer's Month: Participate in activities and campaigns during World Alzheimer's Month in September to raise global awareness.

Support Groups: Establish and promote support groups for caregivers and individuals with Alzheimer's to provide a safe space for sharing experiences and information.

Art and Cultural Events: Organize art exhibitions, film screenings, or cultural events that address Alzheimer's themes and engage the public.

Corporate Partnerships: Collaborate with businesses and organizations to create awareness campaigns, fundraising initiatives, or employee volunteer programs focused on Alzheimer's.

Raising awareness is an ongoing effort that involves individuals, communities, organizations, and policymakers. By working together, we can promote understanding, reduce stigma, and support those affected by Alzheimer's disease in their journey.

Reducing Stigma

Reducing the stigma associated with Alzheimer's disease is essential for creating a more supportive and inclusive environment for individuals living with the condition and their caregivers. Stigma often leads to discrimination, isolation, and barriers to diagnosis and care. Here are some strategies to help reduce the stigma surrounding Alzheimer's:

Education and Awareness: Promote accurate information about Alzheimer's disease through educational campaigns, workshops, and online resources. Clear, fact-based information can dispel misconceptions.

Personal Stories: Encourage individuals and families affected by Alzheimer's to share their personal experiences. Hearing real-life stories can humanize the condition and reduce stereotypes.

Language Matters: Encourage the use of respectful and person-centered language when discussing Alzheimer's. Avoid terms that stigmatize or demean individuals with the condition.

Challenging Myths: Address common myths and misconceptions about Alzheimer's through public awareness campaigns. Provide scientific evidence to counter these myths.

Diverse Representation: Promote diversity and inclusivity in Alzheimer's awareness materials and campaigns to reflect the full range of individuals affected by the disease.

Media Engagement: Work with media outlets to ensure responsible and accurate reporting on Alzheimer 's-related stories, avoiding sensationalism and stigmatizing language.

Involvement of Influential Figures: Engage celebrities, public figures, and community leaders to advocate for Alzheimer's awareness and destigmatization.

Dementia-Friendly Initiatives: Promote the development of dementia-friendly communities that focus on providing support and understanding to individuals with Alzheimer's and their caregivers.

Empathy and Compassion Training: Offer empathy and compassion training to healthcare providers, caregivers, and the general public to help them better understand the experiences of individuals with Alzheimer's.

Support Groups: Facilitate support groups where caregivers and individuals with Alzheimer's can share their challenges, experiences, and strategies for coping. These groups foster understanding and empathy.

Art and Cultural Initiatives: Encourage the use of art, music, theater, and cultural events to challenge stereotypes and promote understanding of Alzheimer's.

Advocacy for Policy Change: Advocate for policies that protect the rights and dignity of individuals with Alzheimer's, such as anti-discrimination laws and increased access to healthcare and support services.

Collaboration with Advocacy Organizations: Partner with Alzheimer's associations and advocacy groups to amplify awareness efforts and share resources.

School and Youth Programs: Integrate Alzheimer's education into school curricula to educate younger generations about the condition and reduce future stigma.

Peer Support: Encourage individuals who have experienced Alzheimer's in their families to provide peer support to others facing similar challenges.

Reducing stigma is an ongoing effort that requires collaboration across society, from individuals and families to healthcare professionals, policymakers, and the media. By raising awareness, challenging stereotypes, and promoting empathy and understanding, we can create a more inclusive and supportive environment for those affected by Alzheimer's disease.

Policy and Funding

Policy and funding play a crucial role in addressing the challenges posed by Alzheimer's disease. Effective policies and adequate funding can support research, improve access to care, and enhance the quality of life for individuals living with Alzheimer's and their caregivers. Here are key aspects related to policy and funding for Alzheimer's:

Research Funding: Governments and private organizations should allocate substantial funding for Alzheimer's research. Research is essential for understanding the disease, developing treatments, and finding a cure.

National Alzheimer's Plans: Many countries have developed national Alzheimer's plans that outline strategies for addressing the disease comprehensively. These plans often include goals related to research, caregiver support, public awareness, and healthcare access.

Access to Early Diagnosis: Policies should promote early diagnosis of Alzheimer's disease, ensuring that individuals receive proper assessments and access to available treatments and support services.

Dementia-Friendly Communities: Policies can encourage the creation of dementia-friendly communities that provide accessible services, support, and understanding to individuals with Alzheimer's and their caregivers.

Caregiver Support: Policies should prioritize support for caregivers, including respite care, training, and financial assistance. Caregivers play a crucial role in caring for individuals with Alzheimer's who need adequate support.

Long-Term Care: Policies should address the need for long-term care options, including home- and community-based services and memory care facilities. These services can help individuals with Alzheimer's live in a safe and supportive environment.

Anti-Discrimination Laws: Laws should protect the rights of individuals with Alzheimer's and their caregivers, including anti-discrimination measures in employment and housing.

Research Incentives: Policies can provide incentives for pharmaceutical companies and researchers to invest in Alzheimer's drug development. These incentives may include tax breaks, grants, or fast-track approval processes.

Public Awareness Campaigns: Government-supported public awareness campaigns can help reduce stigma, raise awareness about Alzheimer's risk factors, and encourage early diagnosis.

Telehealth and Remote Care: Policies should support the use of telehealth and remote care options, especially in rural or underserved areas, to improve access to healthcare for individuals with Alzheimer's.

Collaborative Initiatives: Governments can collaborate with Alzheimer's associations, advocacy groups, and researchers to develop and implement policies that address the complex challenges of Alzheimer's.

International Collaboration: International collaboration and information sharing can accelerate progress in Alzheimer's research and policy development.

Adequate Insurance Coverage: Policies should ensure that health insurance plans provide coverage for Alzheimer 's-related care, including medications, medical visits, and long-term care services.

Support for Caregiver Employment: Policies can encourage workplace flexibility and support for caregivers to balance their caregiving responsibilities with employment.

Ethical Considerations: Policies should address ethical concerns related to Alzheimer's research, including informed consent, data privacy, and the rights of research participants.

Efforts to improve policy and funding for Alzheimer's should be guided by the principles of inclusivity, compassion, and a commitment to finding effective treatments and support systems for those affected by the disease. Engaging with policymakers, advocating for change, and participating in awareness campaigns can all contribute to advancing the cause of Alzheimer's research and care.

Chapter 9

Personal Stories of Resilience

Stories of Individuals Living with Alzheimer's

Sharing the stories of individuals living with Alzheimer's can provide valuable insights into their experiences, challenges, and resilience. These stories help humanize the condition and promote understanding and empathy. Here are a few brief stories to illustrate the diverse experiences of people affected by Alzheimer's:

Sarah's Journey: Sarah was diagnosed with Alzheimer's at the age of 65. Despite the initial shock and fear, she and her family decided to face the disease head-on. Sarah actively participates in support groups and advocacy efforts to raise awareness about Alzheimer's. She emphasizes the importance of living in the present and cherishing each moment with her loved ones.

David's Caregiver Role: David is the primary caregiver for his wife, Emily, who has been living with Alzheimer's for five years. He describes the emotional toll it takes on him and their family but also the profound love and connection that remain strong. David highlights the importance of seeking support and respite to provide the best care possible.

Maria's Passion for Art: Maria, a talented artist, was diagnosed with Alzheimer's in her late 60s. Despite memory challenges, she continues to create beautiful artwork that reflects her emotions and experiences. Her art has become a source of comfort and self-expression, allowing her to communicate when words fail her.

James's Advocacy Efforts: James was diagnosed with early-onset Alzheimer's at 52. Rather than retreating from the world, he became an advocate for Alzheimer's awareness. He shares his story through public speaking and writing, emphasizing the importance of reducing stigma and supporting research.

Lisa's Support Group Connection: Lisa, in her 70s, attends a weekly Alzheimer's support group. She initially felt isolated and overwhelmed by her diagnosis but found solace in connecting with others who understood her challenges. Lisa values the friendships and support she has gained from the group.

These stories highlight the resilience, determination, and humanity of individuals living with Alzheimer's and their caregivers. They also underscore the importance of raising awareness, reducing stigma, and providing support and resources for those affected by the disease. Each person's journey with Alzheimer's is unique, and these stories inspire hope and compassion in the face of adversity.

Their Inspiring Journeys

Here are a few inspiring journeys of individuals living with Alzheimer's:

George's Musical Legacy: **

George, a retired music teacher, was diagnosed with Alzheimer's in his late 70s. Instead of letting the diagnosis deter him, he decided to use his musical talents to connect with others. He started a choir for individuals with dementia, allowing them to create beautiful music together. George's passion for music and his determination to share it have brought joy and a sense of purpose to his life and the lives of others in the choir.

Margaret's Advocacy for Early Diagnosis:

Margaret was diagnosed with Alzheimer's in her early 60s. She became an advocate for early diagnosis and intervention. Margaret shares her story openly, encouraging others to seek help at the first signs of cognitive changes. Her advocacy has led to increased awareness about the importance of early detection and timely access to support and treatments.

Tom's Creative Expression:

Tom, an artist, found that his Alzheimer's diagnosis opened up a new chapter in his artistic journey. He began creating abstract art that reflected his changing perceptions and emotions. Tom's artwork has been exhibited in galleries, and he uses his talent to raise awareness about Alzheimer's and the power of creative expression.

Maria's Travel Adventures:

Maria, who loves to travel, decided not to let Alzheimer's stop her from exploring the world. With the support of her family and careful planning, she continues to embark on trips to new destinations. Maria's determination to keep traveling serves as an inspiration to others with Alzheimer's that life's adventures can continue.

John's Lifelong Learning:
John, a retired professor, has always been passionate about learning. Even after his Alzheimer's diagnosis, he continued to attend lectures, take online courses, and engage in intellectual pursuits. His commitment to lifelong learning not only keeps his mind active but also inspires others to embrace their interests and passions.

These inspiring journeys demonstrate that a diagnosis of Alzheimer's disease doesn't define a person's entire life. Instead, it can be a catalyst for new experiences, creativity, advocacy, and meaningful connections with others. These individuals exemplify resilience, courage, and the power of the human spirit in the face of Alzheimer's challenges.

Conclusion

"Eternal Minds: A Hopeful Exploration of Alzheimer's Disease" is a journey through the intricate landscape of Alzheimer's, a disease that challenges the very essence of who we are. Within these pages, we have ventured into the depths of scientific understanding, traversed the emotional terrain of those affected, and glimpsed the resilience and hope that transcend the limitations of memory.

Throughout this exploration, we have uncovered the multifaceted nature of Alzheimer's. We have delved into the historical context, witnessing how our understanding has evolved from a mysterious affliction to a complex neurodegenerative condition. We have examined the prevalence of the disease and its profound impact on individuals, families, and societies. We have unraveled the intricate anatomy of the brain, delving into the world of neurons, synapses, and proteins. We have explored the role of genetics, the formation of amyloid plaques, the intricacies of tau protein tangles, and the dynamics of inflammation and immune responses in Alzheimer's.

But "Eternal Minds" is not just a dissection of a disease; it is a testament to the enduring spirit of those living with Alzheimer's and the unwavering dedication of caregivers, researchers, and advocates. It is a reminder that even in the face of profound memory loss, the essence of a person endures, their humanity remains intact, and their stories continue to be written.

In the realm of diagnosis and staging, we have confronted the challenges of recognizing cognitive changes, offering a glimpse into the complexities of assessment and the importance of early intervention. Coping strategies have been unveiled, offering a lifeline to those navigating the unpredictable course of Alzheimer's. The perspectives of caregivers have been shared, shedding light on the profound impact of the disease on families and the vital role of support networks.

As we explored the realm of support and resources, we discovered a tapestry of organizations, communities, and initiatives dedicated to providing assistance, education, and comfort to those affected by Alzheimer's. We have witnessed the promising discoveries on the horizon, offering hope that one day we may unlock the secrets of this enigmatic disease.

In the chapters on clinical trials and treatments, we have seen the tireless efforts of researchers and the resilience of participants, reminding us that the pursuit of knowledge and effective therapies continues unabated. In our exploration of preventive measures, lifestyle modifications, and alternative therapies, we have learned that there are proactive steps we can take to promote brain health and potentially reduce the risk of Alzheimer's.

As we conclude this journey through "Eternal Minds," we are left with a profound sense of hope. Hope that science will continue to unravel the mysteries of Alzheimer's. Hope that awareness will reduce stigma and promote understanding. Hope that support networks will grow stronger, and compassionate care will become the standard. Hope that individuals living with Alzheimer's will continue to inspire us with their resilience and courage.

Alzheimer's disease may challenge memory, but it cannot erase the eternal essence of the human spirit. It is a reminder that even in the face of profound adversity, there is hope, there is love, and there is the enduring power of the mind and heart.

As we close this chapter on "Eternal Minds," let it serve as a beacon of hope, a source of knowledge, and a testament to the indomitable spirit of those affected by Alzheimer's. May it inspire us all to continue exploring, advocating, and caring for the eternal minds that grace our lives.

www.ingramcontent.com/pod-product-compliance
Lightning Source LLC
Chambersburg PA
CBHW060952260726
48661CB00005B/1854